Creative Church Bulletin Boards

Rosalind M. Townley

CSS Publishing Company, Inc., Lima, Ohio

CREATIVE CHURCH BULLETIN BOARDS

Library of Congress Cataloging-in-Publication Data

Townley, Rosalind M., 1957-
   Creative church bulletin boards / Rosalind M. Townley.
   p. cm.
   ISBN 0-7880-2359-4 (perfect bound : alk. paper)
1. Bulletin boards in Christian education. I. Title.

BV1535.25.T69 2005
254'.3—dc22

                                                      2004029502

For more information about CSS Publishing Company resources, visit our website at www.csspub.com or e-mail us at custserv@csspub.com or call (800) 241-4056.

Cover design by Chris Patton
ISBN 0-7880-2359-4   PRINTED IN U.S.A.

This book is dedicated to my parents,
who would rather maintain the church's grounds
and balance the budget
than come up with an idea for a bulletin board.

And to my husband and daughters
who live patiently and uncomplainingly
with the clutter of things that are
"just perfect for a bulletin board!"

Table Of Contents

Discovering Your Own Creativity

Preparation —
The Early Stages

Finding An Idea

An interesting bulletin board can be created on almost any topic imaginable. The first step is to find an idea. Don't worry ... it doesn't have to come out of your head. Inspiration is all around you if you know where to look for it.

Scripture

Scripture has inspired people through the centuries to accomplish great and wonderful things. So why not tap into its power and let it inspire *you*? Do you have a favorite verse? Did you hear a particularly meaningful scripture lesson? Use it as a starting point! Can't remember where in the Bible to find it or exactly how it's worded? A concordance can help. If you don't own one of these invaluable references, check your church library or pick up your own paperback copy inexpensively at a local bookstore.

Church Sign Boards

Next time you're out running errands, notice the churches you pass. Most churches have signs out in front telling you the church's name and service times. Many of these churches also include a catchy little slogan or a sermon title, perfect for use on a bulletin board.

Religious Catalogs Or Stores

Even if you are not in the market to buy anything, search through stores and read catalogs thoroughly. There are many opportunities for inspiration here. Read what the T-shirts say. If you are in a store, take time to look at the note paper or read the greeting cards. Look at posters, framed art, and decorative flags. Inspiration doesn't have to start with words, it can come first in the form of a picture that catches your attention. A good visual image often will bring words to mind.

Inspirational Reading Material

Here inspirational does not have to be translated as religious. It *can* be, but it doesn't *have* to be. Many churches offer devotional booklets or pamphlets, and these are a good source of ideas. Just don't limit yourself to them. Some works which aren't expressly considered religious can be very inspirational. Check your local bookstore's inspirational section.

The Internet

If you or someone you know works in an office, school district, or anywhere a sizable group of people have computer and internet access, you've got an idea source. Co-workers sometimes e-mail each other funny jokes, inspirational messages, or food-for-thought ideas that they have come across on the internet. With so many people on "the net" the chance of coming up with something you can use on a bulletin board is much better than if you "surfed the web" yourself looking for ideas.

Sermons / Classes / Conversations

Have you heard an inspiring sermon? Did something in a study group or Sunday school class grab your attention? Have you had a conversation with someone that sparked your interest? Think about the topic. Ponder the thought. Not all great ideas happen instantly. Sometimes successful bulletin boards start with a broad idea. Then, with a little time and some thought, that idea can be refined and narrowed down to make a perfect title or theme for a board.

Music

Music can touch the soul in a way words often can't. Listen to the hymns at church. Borrow a copy of the hymnal and read the words of songs you recognize and some you don't. Lyrics are often designed to fit music, and hymnal music is usually intended to be sung by the average, non-musically trained person. That means that the words come in short, neat, concise little groupings — ready for use just as they are on a bulletin board! Secular music can also be a source of ideas. Try folk music or love songs, after all, "God is love."

Things

Usually the "horse comes before the cart," but occasionally it's the other way around. Let a thing or an item suggest the topic for the board. Do you think a toy hard hat's cute? Use it on a bulletin board about building God's kingdom. How about those rubber grapes? "I am the vine and you are the branches." Do you like something but can't envision what it could become? Ask someone for their input. We don't see all things the same way. Where you draw a blank, someone else might come up with a great idea!

Laying Your Groundwork

Here is where you do some behind-the-scenes planning that will help you not just with your first bulletin board, but with any others that may come later.

Start A File Of Ideas

Okay, so you thought up a good idea. It won't do you any good if you can't remember it when you need it. Right now, start a file of ideas. Use an envelope, use a file folder, use a box, anything that works for you. The important thing is to save those ideas. That way, if you receive a Christmas card that would make a terrific bulletin board, but December's board is already up, file the card. You'll know where to find the idea next year. Rip pictures out of catalogs and magazines. Jot down slogans. Hold on to those internet printouts. An idea file will save you a lot of time. You won't have to waste your energy thinking up an idea when you need one. Just hunt through your file until you find something that's suitable for the occasion or time of year.

11

Know Your Board's Measurements

Now let's think about the bulletin board itself. Know your board's measurements. Don't trust your memory. Write them down somewhere, perhaps in your idea file. It's even a good idea to carry them on a scrap of paper in your wallet or handbag. This can save you trouble down the road. A great idea won't be great if there's not enough room on the bulletin board to fit everything you've planned. By the same token, if you put everything on and you've still got wide expanses of uncovered board, that won't be effective either. Carrying your board's measurements can help you when you're shopping for supplies: "Will I have enough paper?" "Will this neat item fit?" or "Will it take up so much room that there won't be any place to put the words?"

Think Outside The Board

Try to see beyond the rectangle that is your bulletin board. At some point in time you may want to consider designs that will extend beyond the edges of your board. Even if you don't, a hammer and nails can be very helpful. Measure the width of your board's frame. Mark the top of the frame at its center. If your board has a wooden frame, hammer in a nail at this point, making sure it's parallel to the wall (not sticking out toward you). If your board has a metal frame, wedge a nail down between the board and the wall. This nail will serve two purposes. First, it will be a permanent marker of where the bulletin board's center is so that no matter what you are going to put up, you'll be able to center it at a glance. Second, this nail can support anything which you might wish to wrap around the edges of the board. (More on that later.) At this point you will want to add two more nails to the top of the bulletin board frame — one close to each end of the frame. These will provide additional support for anything outside the frame of the board (for example, a garland of flowers).

Choose A Schedule That Works For You

By now you may be anxious to get started. There's still some preliminary planning that needs to be done, and that is: How often will this bulletin board need to be changed? Find a schedule that will work for you and your church. Perhaps your congregation would enjoy a new board every month. Maybe you'll be changing the bulletin board to match the seasons of the church year, or the calendar year. Or maybe your board will be used only to draw attention to special events, to encourage mission giving, or as an outreach to other groups who use your church's facilities. Whatever its purpose, get a feel for how often the board will need to be changed. Knowing this is useful for two reasons. First, as you are shopping for bulletin board supplies, you probably won't want to spend a mint on a bulletin board that will only be displayed for a short time. If, however, the board will be up for a while, the investment might be more worthwhile. Second, if you know how often the board is going to be changed, you can plan ahead — getting an idea, collecting supplies as you see them. This eliminates the stress of trying to collect everything at the last minute. It can also keep the cost down because you can purchase what you are going to need as you see it, hopefully on sale.

Knowing Your Tools

To anyone who's ever even thought about putting up a bulletin board, the first tool to come to mind is a stapler. It's obvious. It's indispensable, and it's also only the tip of the iceberg. The following items all have their place in bulletin board construction, and when used correctly, will do no damage to a standard board.

Stapler
Used to hold up background material and to attach lightweight items to the bulletin board or bulletin board frame (if it's wooden).

Staple Gun
Used like a stapler, the staple gun is capable of holding up items of greater weight. It is also a better choice, if your board has a wooden frame, for stapling items which might extend off your board and onto its frame, for example, flower garlands.

Scissors

Another obvious choice. Useful in cutting materials to size and in cutting out letters. Scissors can also double as a tool to pry stapling mistakes out of a board.

Glue Gun

A glue gun can be used to mount heavier items on your bulletin board. It is also useful in attaching lightweight items through which a staple might not easily pass.

Tape

Scotch, masking, duct, packing, electrical, or colored. If you can think of it, it can be used.

Hammer And Nails

Already mentioned, nails can be used to mark center points as well as to support weight. Just a note here. Think carefully about where you put your nails ... they'll be there to stay. If you attempt to repeatedly remove and replace nails, the holes will become enlarged making them wobbly, unable to support weight and not true indicators of center points.

Exacto Knife

Sometimes an exacto knife works better than scissors when cutting small items or tight curves. (Just remember to put something under it so you don't end up cutting your table top or carpet, too!)

Dental Floss

It's not just for teeth! It's thin, and it can be easily camouflaged behind background material.

Pins

Available at sewing stores, pins can support a fair amount of weight without damaging either the item being mounted or the bulletin board itself. Used in one of two ways, pins can act like staples, piercing an item to attach it to the board. Or they can support an object's weight by being inserted through holes and openings in the object or by being placed under the lower edges of an item so that its weight rests on the pins. Sometimes pins are used in small groupings for increased strength.

Stencils
A definite must for making letters and numbers.

Stencil Machine
This is a luxury, but if you've ever used one you'll never want to go back to tracing and cutting. If your church doesn't own one or can't be convinced to invest in one, do a little investigating. Do you know any teachers who have access to one and might be willing to cut out letters for you? Is there a teacher resource center in your area? Sometimes such centers own stencil machines and will allow use of their equipment for a minimal fee.

Staple Remover
This is a useful tool if you have short fingernails or are concerned that your nails stay in their best possible shape.

Hey, This Is Going To Cost Money!

Any bulletin board you make is going to cost money. At this point there are three questions you should be asking yourself: "How much money am I going to spend on this bulletin board?" "Where is the money going to come from?" and "How can I keep the cost down?"

How Much Should I Spend?

Set A Limit

Choose an amount of money which seems reasonable and try to stick to it. For example, if your figure is ten dollars and it costs four dollars to buy construction paper to cover the board, then you know you've only got six dollars left to work with. Without an awareness of cost, it's easy to exceed your spending limit. This might not matter once or twice, but if you plan to create multiple displays over time, it can run into more money than you planned to spend.

Where Will The Money Come From?

You

If the amount you've settled on is not too high, and if you can afford it, you might think about financing the bulletin board yourself. Look at it as a gift not only of your resources, but also of your time and talents.

A Benefactor

Consider enlisting the financial aid of someone else. If personally financing a bulletin board is beyond your means, find someone who will supplement what you *can* give. Perhaps there is someone who would be willing to pay for *all* the expenses of a bulletin board.

The Church

Is there a general fund from which the money can be drawn? If not, maybe a small amount of financing could be arranged from another area of the church budget. Will the bulletin board be seen by outside groups who can use the church facilities? Money might be made available through an outreach area of the budget.

How Can I Keep The Cost Down?

Now that you've got an idea where the money's coming from, you'll want to make that money go as far as possible. Before purchasing anything, consider your options.

Freebies Or Ask, Ask, Ask

Many interesting things can be acquired without having to hand over a penny. Just remember the importance of a thank you. Express your gratitude up front, of course. But later, photograph your completed bulletin board and take the picture to show the person who helped you. They will appreciate the additional thanks, will enjoy seeing what you did with what they donated, and it will increase the chances that they'll help you again in the future!

Ask Retail Stores

Hanging or freestanding displays often appear with the holidays, seasons, or current promotionals. Once those events have gone by, the decorations are taken down. Sometimes they are saved, but often they are thrown out. Ask — *in advance!* (Teachers and other people know this secret, too. With freebies it's first come, first served.) Don't forget to say that you will be using the materials at your church. Merchants are more willing to give when asked on behalf of a charitable organization. Leave your name and phone number so the store can call you when the displays become available. Be prepared to pick them up on the same day the store calls. While merchants are willing to give away old displays, the key word here is *away*. If you don't take it promptly, someone else will.

Ask Specialty Shops

Want posters of interesting places? Ask a travel agent. Would some giant hard candies look cute on your board? Ask a dry cleaner for a couple of plastic bags for making wrappers. Texture and color always add to a bulletin board. Ask your local wallpaper dealer for old sample books. Want to make some trees or bushes? Florist's green tissue paper works well. And don't forget supermarkets. They often have seasonal displays just like other retail stores, but since they're in the business of storing food, they usually don't bother with storing displays.

Ask People

Have you got a great idea for a bulletin board, but can't use it because you're missing something to complete it? Ask! Ask your family. Ask your friends. Ask your congregation. Someone's bound to know where to get it. Maybe they'll donate the item. Maybe they'll loan it. Either way, there's no out-of-pocket expense.

Really Cheap Stuff

Recycle, reuse, reinvent. It may cost you a bit to buy a roll of colored bulletin board paper, but you should be able to cover more than one board with it. Consider also that cost averaging can actually make it quite inexpensive. Use it this month as background material. When you take the paper down, it will have holes in it. So save the larger pristine sections to cut out, for example, flowers for next month. When you're done with the flowers, use them for cutting out letters. Did you make a nice treetop from the florist's tissue? It can be recycled into a bush and later into grass.

Cheap Stuff

There are many varied places where materials may be obtained cheaply for your bulletin board. Dollar stores are a good start. When nothing costs over one dollar, you can buy a lot and not go over your budget. If the season's right, yard sales are another gold mine. (Here's your chance to let a thing decide what direction your theme will take!) Prices are usually both cheap and negotiable and there's

18

no telling what neat things you might find. Out of "yard sale season" try resale and discount stores. The prices aren't as good as yard sales, but the merchandise is often as interesting and eclectic. Party stores are a place to find interesting and useful items, but usually nothing too large. These stores are specialty stores and their pricing reflects that. Lastly, remember that all stores have sales, even dollar stores. Don't forget to check for bargains on seasonal merchandise once its season has gone by.

The Expensive Stuff
Occasionally indulging in something expensive is not a bad thing. There are times when something special can really make the difference between a good bulletin board and an extraordinary one. The overall cost for your bulletin board can still be kept down by completing the board with supplies that are recycled or very inexpensive.

19

The Idea Becomes Reality

Beyond Construction Paper

It goes almost without saying that construction paper is a basic bulletin board component. But construction paper alone is about as interesting as a birthday cake without the icing, decorations, and candles. A really eye-catching bulletin board needs color and texture. These two things can be added in a number of ways.

Backgrounds

Of course sheets or rolls of construction paper make excellent material for covering your board. But why not be more imaginative? Not ready to try anything too exotic? Use gift wrap or wallpaper. Corrugated cardboard comes on rolls for use on bulletin boards. You can find solid colors or a variety of prints such as bricks. Ready to be a little less traditional? Try using plastic tablecloths. Fabric or felt off the bolt can look very nice. If you're feeling especially bold or are striving for a special effect, try cellophane, sandpaper, or even bubble wrap.

Borders — Inside And Out

If you plan to put a border around the inside of your bulletin board, there are two styles of pre-made borders which are readily available. These are the traditional, corrugated cardboard scalloped edging, and the newer, straight-edged picture borders. Depending on how you use them, these can look nice. The drawback is that they take up space which otherwise might be used for the main theme of your board. Your second option is to put a border around the outside of your board. Want a traditional look? Paper chains work nicely. Ready to be a little more daring? Strands of silk flowers or leaves look pretty. Garland, like you might find on a Christmas tree, comes in many colors and is light and easy to put up. Netting, available at fabric stores, can give a bunting effect. Ribbon can be used in a continuous length off the spool or can be made into bows to mount on the four corners of your board's frame. If your board is near an electrical outlet, you can even outline your board with Christmas lights!

The Main Show
What you choose to display on the main section of your bulletin board will depend on what the theme is. The possibilities are almost limitless ... if you can imagine it, you can do it. Start simple. Try paper plates, cotton balls, or foam. Going with a summer theme? Add a beach towel. Thinking about rain showers? Use an old umbrella with one side flattened. Is it spring or fall? Bunches, single stems, or garlands of silk flowers or fall leaves add realism. Planning a picnic board? Why not add rubber fruit or plastic bugs? Going with a celebration theme? Mylar balloons stay aloft for a long time. Even stuffed animals can be used on a bulletin board. (**Very important note:** If you should decide to enlist the help of these gentle creatures, please be kind. Teddies and their animals friends are *not* "into" body piercing. When placing them on a bulletin board, *never* staple body parts! You can staple tags, clothes, even fur, but never ears, tails, or toes!)

How In The Heck Am I Supposed To Put *That* Up?

Now that you know *what* you want to put on your bulletin board, the trick is figuring out *how* to put it there. There are multiple techniques which you can employ. Sometimes you may want to use just one. Other times, depending on what you're planning to mount, a combination of techniques may work better.

Remember Your Nails
Now is the time that those nails you hammered or wedged in come into play. If you're putting up borders, things like garland and silk flowers can be tucked behind the nails at the top of the board, and either stapled (on wood frames) or taped (on metal frames) at the bottom of the board. Nails can be used to hang corner decorations, like bows. If you are up for a challenge, nails can

also be used to support some of the weight of an object elsewhere on the board. (This particular use of nails is probably the most complicated method of mounting objects that will be discussed here. Don't panic. It's really not as bad as it sounds. If after reading it you think it's not for you, don't worry. There will be plenty of easier options later.)

Before you put up your background material, decide on the item you want to hang, and where you want it to go. Cut a length of string, dental floss, or fishing line that will reach, with extra to spare, from your object to the nail. Attach one end of the string to the item, either through a hole or by hot gluing or taping it to the underside of the object. Make a lasso-type loop at the opposite end of the string. Hang the loop over the nail. Now place the item to be mounted against the bulletin board, checking to see if, when the string is taut, the object is where you want it to be. If not, adjust the loop to lengthen or shorten the string. When the length is right, it's time to staple. Hold your item in one hand, keeping the string taut. With a stapler in the other hand, liberally staple along the length of the string. Once done, slowly and gently release your grip on the item you're mounting. Hopefully, it will stay in place.

Now all that remains is to "cover your tracks." This is done by putting up your construction paper background as usual. The paper will also serve to keep the string in place. If you're concerned that the item you've just mounted still needs a little more support, put some pins under the object to help hold its weight. Still worried? Add a few staples to the paper along the track of the string ... that object won't be going anywhere!

Don't Forget Your Frame

Depending on the layout of your board, larger items can be made to extend off the edges of the board. Then the board's frame itself can help support the weight of the item. This works especially well on boards with wooden frames. Your item can now be stapled with a staple gun right onto the frame. Staple gun staples are stronger than regular staples. Because they are applied by the mechanical pressure of the staple gun, they fit more tightly up against the frame and will hold items more securely. The only downside to this is that because they fit so snugly, they are harder to remove than standard staples. A metal frame may not be as useful as a wooden one for supporting weight, but don't overlook the possibility of using tape or magnets on it.

Use The Floor

Not everything has to be *on* the bulletin board to be part of it. Doing a summer bulletin board on the theme "Fishers of men"? Set a fishing rod on the floor and lean it up against the board. Let the floor carry some of the weight of a tall display. If your board includes a tree with a cardboard trunk, make it a long one. The bottom of the trunk can sit on the floor and help support the weight of the upper branches.

Aim Your Glue Gun

Relatively light items can be hot glued directly to the background of the board. *Don't* use this option if you've chosen plastic or cellophane for your background as it will melt. Want to make the hot glue dry faster? Set a blow dryer on its "cool" setting and aim it at the melted glue. If you're worried about the background paper tearing, give your item a little extra support by stapling an outline closely around your object. Heavier items can be attached to a bulletin board with hot glue, but an extra step is required. First, hot glue the item to a piece of poster board. Then, as with the string and nail technique, staple the poster board to the bulletin board *before* the background paper goes up. You can use regular staples, a staple gun, or a combination of the two, depending on the thickness of your poster board and the weight of the item being mounted. Finally, as before, cover your tracks with construction paper.

Don't Overlook The Wall

As mentioned before, lightweight items can extend beyond the rectangle of the board. Sometimes extending an item to the border is far enough, but on other occasions, further could be better. You might even want to (temporarily) put things on the wall that are separate from the bulletin board. A word to the wise: Be careful what you use to put up such decorations. Use masking tape sparingly or check with an office supply store to see what's available that can be removed easily. Your church's trustees will not be happy if you pull paint off the wall when your bulletin board comes down!

"It Is Finished" — Or Is It?

Congratulations! You did it! Your bulletin board is done. Or is it? If you will be responsible for creating more than just this one bulletin board, then "done" is not a word that should be in your vocabulary. "Temporarily finished" may be more like it. Once you have put in the last staple, thrown out your paper scraps, and put away your scissors, it's time to start all over again. Think about the next board's theme. Start collecting and shopping for your supplies. If you're not using a stencil machine and know what your theme will be, begin cutting your letters now. That way you won't end up with hand cramps from having to cut them all at once at the last minute. In short, do all the advance preparation you can for the next "upcoming attraction." The more you do now, the easier the job will be next time.

Still feel like you need some help creating bulletin boards? Trust your own creativity, but read on!

Help!
I Don't
Have Any
Creativity!

Otherwise Known As
"I Skipped Part One"

Instant Creativity

Okay, so you're very busy and didn't have time to read part one. Or maybe you really did read it, but still feel your creativity could use a jump start. This section can help.

The ideas that follow will be arranged, for ease of reference, in two sections. Within each section, general themes will come first. Next will be a selection of specific phrases relating to the themes. Finally, one phrase will be shown as it was used on an actual bulletin board. Information relating to supplies and mounting techniques will be included should you choose to recreate the sample board.

The first section will cover the calendar year, including both religious and secular holidays. At this point you might be asking yourself why secular holidays would be included in a book about church bulletin boards. The answer is simple ... children! Children are the future of our churches and even the youngest child seems to be aware of holidays. So why not capitalize on that? Create a bulletin board with a holiday appearance which conveys a religious message!

The second section will include general themes. These themes will be suitable for use at any time during the year.

The Calendar Year

January

Themes

Resolutions, new beginnings, snow

Specific Phrases

"Though your sins be scarlet, they shall be as white as snow"; "200_ (fill in appropriate year number) ... Time to look to Jesus" (let the 00s be giant eyes); In Christ ... all things are become new"

The Board

This board was covered with solid blue gift wrap. (Any blue paper would do, but construction paper would probably not produce so bold a blue.) Gift wrap was also used for the gold letters. The white letters were cut from construction paper, but plain white printer paper works just as nicely. The snowman and the snow across the bottom of the board were cut from quilt batting which was stapled to the board. Available at fabric stores, batting comes either pre-cut in packages or cut to specifications off a bolt.

The trees are small, real tree branches which have had glitter applied to them with liquid glue. Once the glue had dried, the branches were simply slipped behind the batting. The little red birds, purchased at a craft store, were tucked into the branches. A small bird was placed on the snowman's head by tucking its feet behind the snowman's head. (The toes caught in the batting and kept the bird from falling.) For a finishing touch, a few gold gummed stars were added to the background and blue garland was wrapped around the board's frame. The garland was held in place by nails at the top (as discussed in the "tool" section of the book) and staples at the bottom.

February

Themes

The heart, love, Valentine's Day

Specific Phrases

"Beloved: Let us love one another because love is from God" — 1 John 4:7; "Let God's love bubble up in your heart" (use bubble wrap); "Our prayers ... conversation hearts for God"; "'Tis so sweet to trust in Jesus"

The Board

The highlight of February's board was a 3-D, heart-shaped box of chocolates. This took a lot of work and will be, by far, the most complicated bulletin board discussed here. If you don't feel up to the challenge of creating a similar box, the board can still be reproduced. By making the box flat while leaving everything else the same, the work is considerably reduced. The remaining items still provide plenty of depth and texture. Directions will be given for creating both boards. Those directions that apply *only* to the 3-D board will appear in *italics*. When preparing this bulletin board, it is advisable to leave yourself plenty of work time in advance of when you want to display the board. The chocolates and their box are created in steps and time must be allowed for glue and paint to dry between the steps.

To make the top of the box of chocolates (either flat or raised), cut a heart shape in a size that is suitable for your board from a large piece of cardboard, such as an appliance box. Cut another heart of the same size from a piece of pink poster board. This will be the bottom of the box.

If you plan to make a 3-D box, the next step is to cut four cardboard strips, two-inches wide, each the length of half the heart's outside edge. To find this measurement, use string to trace the outline of the heart from the point at the bottom of the heart, around the outside and up to the deepest point of the V at the top. Mark the string, remove it from the heart and measure exactly how much you've used. The number you get is the length that your cardboard strips will need to be. Add an inch or two to this number to allow for any measuring mistakes that might have happened. You can always trim the excess off, but you can't make cardboard grow! Cut out the cardboard strips.

Now you are ready to glue. Two of the strips will be glued to the back of the cardboard heart. Using a glue gun, at about a quarter of an inch in from the edge, run a thick line of glue around the back of half of the heart, starting at the point at the bottom and working your way around to the V at the top. While the glue is still hot and soft, hold a cardboard strip perpendicular to the heart and press the narrow edge into the glue. Hold it in place while the

glue dries. (This process can be sped up by blowing on the glue.)
Trim off any excess cardboard which extends beyond the top or
bottom points. Repeat the gluing process again on the opposite
half of the heart so that when you are done, the cardboard strips
meet at the points of both top and bottom. You can reinforce your
glue job by running another line of glue around the inside of the
cardboard strips where they touch the heart. Now it's time to re-
peat the whole gluing process using the pink poster board and the
remaining two cardboards strips. The only difference is that the
second pair of cardboard strips will go on the front *of the* poster
board.

Once your cardboard heart (either flat or raised) is ready, the
next step is to spray paint it pink. Only the top needs to be painted.
If you have chosen to make a 3-D heart, don't forget to paint the
cardboard strips which make up the sides. Try to do this out of
doors if you can. There's better ventilation and you won't need to
worry so much if your aim is less than perfect. Once the paint has
dried, use a small paintbrush and a small bottle of red acrylic paint
(available at craft stores), to paint the word "LOVE" on the top of
the box. Silk roses may be added with a glue gun, as can a lace
ruffle. If you need help deciding how much lace to buy, read (*or*
reread) the section above in italics which explains how to measure the outline of the heart. When you're ready to glue, don't try
to apply all the lace at once. Hot glue dries quickly. Instead, lay
down a line of glue, about six inches in length, right along the top
edge of the heart. Press the lace into it and wait for the glue to set
somewhat. Continue working your way around the heart in this
manner until the whole heart has been outlined in lace.

Now to the chocolates. There are two basic varieties of chocolates on this bulletin board ... those which are made from pom-
poms and those which are made from small gift boxes such as one
in which earrings might come. The pom-poms can be used singly,
just as they are. They can also be hot glued tightly together in
pairs with a small silk flower wedged into the glue between them
to simulate icing roses. More variety can be achieved by using
light brown pom-poms for milk chocolate and dark brown for dark
chocolate!

To make chocolates from gift boxes, choose either light or dark brown felt and wrap the boxes as you would with gift wrap. The felt is held in place by hot glue. To imitate the little squiggle often seen on the tops of fancy chocolates, add a squiggle of brown fabric paint (available inexpensively at craft stores in small, fine-point squeeze bottles). The total number of chocolates you need to make is dependent upon the size of your box. Remember that as the box top and bottom overlap, you do not need to fill the entire box, only the exposed portion, and some of that will be taken up by empty wrappers. (The bulletin board in the picture required seventeen chocolates and three wrappers.) Next, the chocolates need to be glued into their wrappers, which are foil cupcake liners. (Paper liners work, but when you glue the chocolates in, be careful that the glue doesn't soak through the paper and glue the chocolate to your work surface.) Using your hot glue gun, put a large blob of glue in the bottom of the liner. Press the chocolate into the glue and hold it until the glue has set.

The final step in creating the box is to glue the chocolates in place. To determine where the chocolates look best, lap the box top over the box bottom as it will be displayed. If you have chosen to make a flat box, trace with a pencil the outline where the hearts overlap and then remove the box top. Arrange your chocolates on the section of the box bottom which will be exposed and then glue them, and any empty liners you want, in place.

If you have made the 3-D box, lap the top over the bottom, as above, and mark with pencil the two places on the lower cardboard strips where the upper cardboard strips touch. Remove the top and with an exacto knife, on the lower cardboard strips, slice straight down (as if cutting a piece of cake) to a depth of two-thirds to three-fourths of the way through the cardboard strips. Bring the top back and, to check the fit, wedge it down onto the box bottom. If necessary, remove the top and widen your slits. Be very *careful to widen them only as little as is absolutely necessary. The pressure of the two halves being wedged together is* all *that will be holding up your box top when it is mounted! As above, place and glue your chocolates.*

Now comes the easy part: putting up the board. This bulletin board has been covered with pink construction paper. The letters were cut from white construction paper and metallic red poster board. Hanging on the nails at the upper corners are two red velvet bows which were actually salvaged from Christmas wreaths, but yours can be bought or made from any ribbon of your choice. The chocolate box has been mounted by stapling the box bottom to the bulletin board. Staple in multiple places around and in between the chocolates to assure a secure hold. When the bottom is secure, the top is lapped over it, along the outline you traced and stapled. You will find that a staple gun works better than a regular stapler since you are stapling through cardboard. *If you are mounting a 3-D box, mount the bottom as above, then wedge the top in place.* To finish the board, empty cupcake liners have been added. In each of them has been placed, as they were stapled, a short Bible promise: "I will give you rest," "I love you," "My grace is sufficient," or "I forgive you."

This bulletin board requires a lot of time and work, but it really is worth the effort. You'll find that your congregation will respond quite well to the display. In fact, you may hear complaints when this board comes down. You'll probably get requests for a repeat appearance next year. People seem to love it because, after all, God sends no stress that prayer and chocolate can't handle!

March

Themes

Saint Patrick's Day, treasure, luck, wind, midwinter

Specific Phrases

"The pot of gold at the end of God's rainbow" (fruits of the Spirit); "Midwinter blues? Dump your cares on Jesus" (draw a big dump truck); "Do not store up for yourselves treasure on earth. Store up for yourselves treasure in heaven"

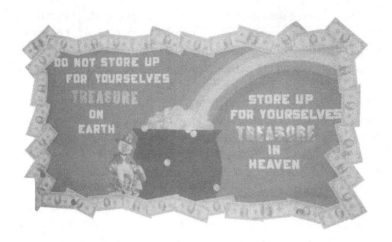

The Board

The green background on this bulletin board is especially vibrant because a roll of fade-resistant bulletin board paper was used. The leprechaun is a holiday cutout, available at party stores or in most regular stores when Saint Patrick's Day is approaching. The leprechaun's pot was cut from a single sheet of black poster board. Shiny gold wrapping paper was used to cut out the word "treasure" and also the gold with which the pot is filled. No specific coin shapes were cut, just a general scalloped edge. The lower edge does not need to be neatly shaped at all as it can be concealed behind the pot. The mountain of gold in the pot was given definition and made more realistic by the addition of cardboard gold coins, purchased at a dollar store. More coins were stapled to the front of the pot to give the appearance that the pot was full to overflowing. Finally, extra coins were added to the board's boarder which was first covered completely in a random pattern with play money (bills), also purchased at a dollar store. White construction paper was used to make the letters (other than "treasure") and the board was completed with the addition of a rainbow.

The rainbow is cut, in curved strips, from five different colors of poster board. Using the following method, it is easy to make curves that fit together nicely. Take the color of poster board that you intend to be at the bottom of the rainbow. Put a pencil in your hand and plant your elbow on your work surface. You will be using your arm as a giant compass. Without moving your elbow, and keeping your hand and arm stiff as you go, move the pencil across the poster board. (The pencil will be writing somewhat on its side instead of in a straight up and down fashion.) Keep moving your arm until you have drawn an arc the size you need. This will probably be a little larger than one-fourth of a circle.

Underneath this line you will next draw a second arc. This can be done by measuring, at regular intervals, down from the line approximately two inches and making a dot. Connect the dots and cut out along the lines you have just drawn. You will have a nice, two-inch wide curved strip which will be the bottom color of your rainbow. To make the next higher color strip, lay the curved piece you just made onto the proper color. Trace the *upper* curve onto the new color. This new line will be the *lower* curve of the second color and will, when cut, fit snugly against the bottom color. The upper curve of this second color can be made by measuring *up* from your line, making your marks, drawing a line, and cutting it out.

Continue in this fashion with each color until all the color strips have been cut. As you get higher up in the colors, the strips will get longer. You may find you have to piece one or two strips — meaning tape or staple two pieces of the same color end to end in order to allow the curve to reach its full width. When all the strips have been cut, staple them to the board. Where the strips end tells you where to place your pot of gold.

April

Themes
Palms, the cross, Easter — both religious (empty tomb, lilies) and secular (Easter baskets, bunnies, eggs), April showers

Specific Phrases
"Thy will be done" ... "He lives" (These make a nice *pair* of boards. Mount a cross on poster board. Cover the bulletin board

37

with purple paper. Then cover over the purple, so that none shows, with black paper. Mount the poster board. Add the first phrase. When Good Friday's past, tear down the black to expose the purple. Remove the old phrase, add one or two silk lilies and the words of the second phrase. Voila! Two different boards for very little work.) "Gone to see Dad. We're fixin' a place for you. Be back soon to pick you up" (a note pinned to a cross); "Hallelujah"; "What if we never saw another flower because we grumbled when God sent rain?"

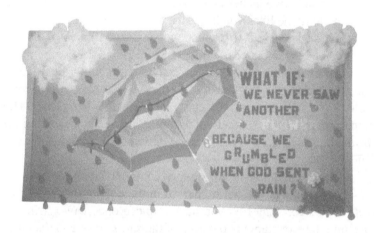

The Board

Despite its complicated appearance, this is a very easy board to put up. The background is covered with gray construction paper. The clouds are fiberfill (usually used to stuff pillows and toys, available in bags at fabric stores). The fiberfill has been stretched out to extend beyond the confines of the board, and stapled, both on the board and on the frame. If you prefer, cotton balls can be used in the same manner, but the clouds won't be as fluffy.

The raindrops were cut from clear blue vinyl, obtained from a bolt at the local fabric store, and stapled randomly to the board and its frame. The small silk flower in the corner has been stapled in place and its stem hidden by a handful of Easter grass, also stapled. Black construction paper was used for all the letters except "flower," which was done in random bright colors.

The focal point of the board is an umbrella. While the umbrella was open, the spokes on one side were bent down, making that side somewhat flat. The flat side of the umbrella was then held up to the bulletin board and copiously stapled. A standard stapler was used. Once the umbrella was in place, a few extra raindrops were stapled around its bottom, as if dripping off. A few others were scotch-taped higher up to look like they were running down.

May

Themes
Spring, Mother's Day

Specific Phrases
"Spring is God's music" (put the phrase on a music staff, make flowers with musical notes for centers, add singing birds); "Sometimes faith means sticking your neck out" (a tree with a hole in the trunk and a small animal peeking out); "Pleasant words are like the honeycomb, sweetness to the soul and health to the body" — Proverbs 16:23 (bumble bees); "All I have seen teaches me to trust the Creator for all I have not seen." — Ralph Waldo Emerson

The Board

This bulletin board truly exemplifies how Christ works in our lives: We offer the lives that we have, faded and dirty with sin, and Christ gives us new life and makes us beautiful. Used artificial flowers for the board were solicited from the church's congregation. The blossoms received, while given with the best of intentions, were a sorry sight: dirty, faded, drooping, and mismatched. And yet, when used on the bulletin board they came together, making an amazingly lovely display to which the picture does not do full justice.

Almost nothing on this board was new. The background is the same green fade-resistant bulletin board paper that was used on March's board. The bush had been recycled from a tree top which was made in the following manner.

Out of cardboard, cut a bush of a suitable size and shape for your board. Spray paint only the front green. While waiting for the paint to dry, cut florist's tissue paper into long strips about two inches wide. Then cut the strips to make squares of about two inches. Exact measurement is not necessary. (Green tissue paper may be used in place of florist's tissue, but it will not hold up as well. Florist's tissue has a thin, waxy coating on it which makes it both sturdier and slows the fading process.) If your paint has dried, take a pencil and center its eraser on one of the squares of paper. Gather the paper up around the pencil, being careful not to poke the pencil through the tissue. Finally, while still holding the pencil and tissue in one hand, use your free hand to place a drop of hot glue anywhere you like on the front of the cardboard bush. Quickly push the tissue-covered eraser into the glue and then remove the pencil, leaving only the tissue paper behind.

Continue working in this fashion, moving outward from your first piece of tissue paper, until you have covered the front of the bush as thickly as you like with paper. Since you will be using hot glue, almost as soon as you have placed the final square of tissue, the bush will be ready to hang.

The bush shown here was allowed to overlap the edges of the bulletin board, so it was attached by a staple gun to the frame of the board. If you have a metal frame or have created a smaller bush, it can be mounted within the board's frame, still using a staple gun.

The grass at the bottom of the board, to the right of the bush, is evergreen-colored Christmas garland. (If you haven't planned ahead, ask. Perhaps someone can provide you with this type of garland. If not, check in your area for a year-round Christmas shop where you might be able to acquire some.) The garland was stapled to the board, starting at the lower right corner. It was run along the bottom of the board, just inside the frame, over to the bush, where it was stapled. There it made a U-turn and went back to the right side of the board. This second row of garland ran just above the first. The pattern was repeated until the grass reached the desired depth. The donated flowers were then tucked into the grass. Some had a (regular) staple or two added if they needed help standing up straight. A few of the flowers were slid in behind the top of the bush, and again, stapled if needed. The last of the used, donated flowers were stapled to the front of the bush at the bottom.

A few extra flowers were added to brighten the board since many of the donated flowers were either pastel or faded. The flowers draped across the top and down the sides of the board were four chains which came from a dollar store. They were tucked behind the center and corner nails in the board's frame. The red flowers, visible in the bush, were silk boutonnieres bought at a yard sale. They were tucked into the tissue of the bush and stapled as needed. This same effect can be achieved by adding a few carnations (just the blooms, no stems). The blue flowers, seen on the bush and two in the grass, were recycled. Previously they had been a plastic tablecloth background.

To create the blue flowers, the tablecloth was cut into four-inch squares. Six squares were stacked one on top of the other. This stack was then folded fan-style — front to back, front to back — until a narrow but thick strip of plastic remained. The strip was next turned onto its side so that the folds faced upward. The plastic was secured in the middle by a twist-tie, the kind that comes with non-zippered food storage bags. The tie was laid across the folds, bent down around the flat sides, and tightly twisted underneath to hold the plastic in place. Finally, holding the twist-tie stem in one hand, each layer of plastic was carefully separated and fluffed up to create a flower. This was all done out of a desire to reduce trash and to conserve finances. If your bulletin board is well financed, or if you don't have the time to invest, all the steps involved in creating the blue flowers can easily be eliminated by just buying blue flowers. These would be applied, like the red flowers, without their stems. Finally, the bulletin board was finished with the quote, which was cut from gold Xerox paper, and by the addition of a butterfly. The butterfly was obtained free at a card store, having once been part of a display. A similar butterfly might easily be purchased at a party supply store.

This bulletin board is *not* as much work as it sounds, especially if you choose not to make your own blue flowers. (You might want to remember the process, though, as it can be used to make not just flowers, but anything which might need a fluffy texture.) The most complicated component of the board, the bush, can be saved and reused, either whole or cut into parts, on another board.

June, July, August

Themes

These three months are grouped together because they share the common themes of summer, hot weather, swimming, ice cream, and picnics. In June, Father's Day is a topic worth considering and July holds patriotic possibilities. The summer months are traditionally a time when people go away on vacation. If you expect that a fair number of your congregation will not be around to appreciate the work that goes into a bulletin board, you might want to consider giving your creativity a rest. Choose one theme suitable for all three summer months and leave it up.

Specific Phrases

June: "What a father drives may change ... what drives him to the Father shouldn't" (use pictures of antique cars and sleek sports cars)

July: "This is my song: a song of peace for lands afar and mine"

Any month: "Summer 'Sundaes' in worship, a sweet treat" (ice cream sundae dish); "Take time to be holy" (a beach scene with a clock's hands and numbers placed on it); "This summer share the faith"

The Board (summer-themed)

This bulletin board is quick and easy. To look a little more like grass, the board was covered with felt from a bolt. If you don't want to spend the money on felt, you could just as easily reuse last month's green paper. The picnic blanket is a piece of gift wrap stapled to the board. If you can't find similar paper, use a pattern that pleases you. Better yet, choose a piece of fabric. The picnic goods really *are* standard picnic supplies: paper plates, napkins, and cups, which were stapled onto the tablecloth. The plastic utensils were just placed in an upright paper cup and required no staples or glue. Additional picnic supplies were placed in a lightweight basket that was stapled, by a staple gun, to the lower left corner of the board's fame. If you have a metal-framed board, either staple within the board's frame, or choose a larger basket and set it on the floor. Remember, not everything that's part of the board has to

43

be attached to it. The hamburger and hot dog are cutouts, and the ants are plastic. They were all obtained at a party store. The ants were stapled on the board with their feet touching the food, and the food was positioned off the tablecloth to give the impression that the ants were carrying the food off to *share*. The flower garland is making a return from May's display. It was draped from the nail at the top center of the board's frame, around the nail at the left top, and allowed to freely dangle down the side of the bulletin board. The blue letters are bright in color because they were cut from fade-resistent bulletin board paper. Nothing, however, would be wrong with using ordinary construction paper, as was the case with the black letters.

The Board (patriotic-themed)

Bold and eye-catching, this bulletin board is another one that does not require a lot of work. It doesn't even call for a lot of supplies. The whole board was covered with red gift wrap. Next, adding machine tape was used to create the white stripes, of which there are six. If you have a good "eye," you can approximate where the adding machine tape will need to be placed to make the stripes.

If not, you can calculate where to place the tape using the following method. Measure the width of the tape. Multiply that number by six, the number of stripes. This answer tells you the total amount of the background that will be covered by white. Subtract your answer from the measurement of the total height of the board. The answer you get will be the number of inches of red background that will become the stripes. Now divide that number by seven and you have the width for each red stripe.

Using the number you got for the red strip width, measure down from the top of the board on each side and make a small mark. This mark will indicate where the top of the first strip of white paper will go. At this point it's helpful to have someone assist you. Place the tape up against one side of the board at the spot you marked. Staple only once at the top and bottom, just enough to hold the tape temporarily in place. Now unroll the adding machine tape across the board to the board's opposite side and line it up with the mark you previously put there. Cut the strip off the roll. While you hold the strip in place, have your helper step back and check to be sure that the stripe is level. Once it is, staple the end in place and then continue to anchor the stripe with staples, working across the paper strip until you reach your starting point.

Next, measure down the width of the next red stripe, and using the same process, place the next white stripe. At this point, even the flag's short stripes will go all the way across the bulletin board. This method assures that the stripes are straight. The stripes will all be shortened at once with the addition of the blue panel, which on this board was cut from gift wrap. To find the height of the blue paper, measure from the top of the board down to the top of the fourth white stripe, as on a real flag, this is where the blue field stops. As for the width of the blue area, you will need to judge what seems appropriate, based on the size of your individual board.

The stars were made by using a star-shaped paper punch, available at craft stores and currently popular for use in making scrapbooks. The stars used on this board were punched from sticky-backed labels. The backing was peeled off and the stars were placed on the blue field. This method avoids the use of staples, which makes for a neater appearance, but is very tedious and time consuming. Peeling the backing off the very narrow points of the stars is not only hard, but it also has a tendency to wrinkle the stars. The advantage, however, is that you can lay the stars on the paper to check their placement and then permanently position them *before* you have mounted the blue paper on the board. If you prefer not to deal with peeling adhesive paper, stars cut from construction paper or copy machine paper can be substituted. You will, of course, need to attach the stars with staples. Just remember that because the neck of a stapler is short and cannot reach very far into the blue field, the stars will have to be added *after* the blue has been mounted, which means you cannot lay out all the stars to check their placement before attaching them.

As for the placement of the stars, there are nine rows. The top row contains six stars, as does every alternate row below it, making a total of five rows. In each of the four rows which fall in between, there are five stars. The placement of so many stars would be time-consuming to measure. Instead, place the stars "by eye" using a few basic guides. Since there are nine rows, the fifth row will fall in the center, with four rows above it and four below. Looking at the stars as columns, there are eleven. That means the sixth column will be the center with five columns on either side. Knowing this gives a general guide for the arrangement of the stars. This bulletin board was completed by the addition of a line of lyrics from a choir anthem. The words were cut from black construction paper.

September

Themes

Returning after summer vacation, "Back to school"

Specific Phrases

"Welcome back to one of fall's blessings ... you"; "1 cross + 3 nails = 4 given"; "Back to Sunday school savings"

The Board

This bulletin board makes use of all the back-to-school advertising — literally! The board is randomly covered with colored advertisements for school supplies. The papers have been allowed to extend beyond the frame of the board and were gently taped to the wall. A giant price tag was cut from three pieces of poster board which had been slightly overlapped and glued together end-to-end. The phrase "Back to Sunday school savings*" was added. With the exception of the letter *S* in Sunday and in savings, all the letters were cut from black construction paper. The two *S*s were made of shiny green paper to suggest dollar signs. The strike throughs on the dollar signs were made from paper supermarket bags cut in the shape of crosses.

To finish the bulletin board, a piece of yellow poster board was used. Cut into two shapes, the first piece is generally round but with many points sticking out from it, somewhat like a sun. It is intended to suggest the attention-grabbing format used by many ads. Hand-lettered in this shape is the phrase, "Christ paid the price!" The sign was placed in the upper right corner of the board. The second piece of yellow poster board is a small rectangle located at the bottom. Also hand-lettered, it has the ad's fine print as denoted by the asterisk. It reads, "Prices effective through eternity."

47

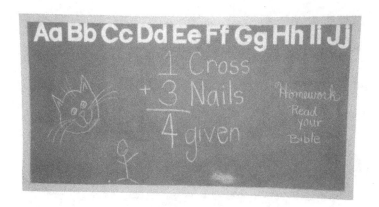

The Board (alternate theme)

This school-themed bulletin board is highly effective, but is as cheap and easy as they come. The board has been covered with black construction paper. Starting with the letter *A*, an upper and lower case letter was cut for as many letters as it took to cover the top width of the board. This particular board called for ten pairs of letters, but depending on the size of the letters you're working with and the width of your board, your requirements may be different. Once you have cut a sufficient number of letters, mount them across the top of the board. Next, write the message, "1 cross + 3 nails = 4 given" with chalk, just as you would on a real chalkboard. If you make a mistake, just erase it and write over it. After all, real chalkboards always have chalk smears on them! Finish off the board by adding any drawings, intentional erasures, or words that you would like. To this particular board was added "Homework: Read your Bible." Keep in mind that younger children may not be able to read cursive writing. Printing may be your best choice for any messages you write on the chalkboard.

October

Themes

Fall, Halloween

According to recent research, Halloween ranks second only to Christmas as one of our country's most popular holidays. This can pose a dilemma for Christians (and for Christian bulletin boards!). It used to be that Halloween meant dressing up in a cowboy costume and collecting candy. Today, the holiday seems to have become the domain not of children, but of adults, and like so much of our society, Halloween has left behind the innocence of earlier times. The once good-natured fun of the holiday has been replaced by a more sinister image. Each successive Halloween seems to strive to be more shocking and more gruesome. Yet, children still love Halloween.

In creating an October bulletin board it *is* still possible to use Halloween as a theme. The trick is to use images which are innocent, either God-created or man-made. Some clear choices are pumpkins, candy, or spiders with webs. Some less obvious choices which require more care in their presentation are bones (with a reference to Ezekiel), blood (concerning "the blood of the Lamb"), and cemeteries (mentioned below).

Specific Phrases

"Sweet Trinity ... Three in one" (a giant candy corn with the words "Father," "Son," and "Holy Ghost" each written on a different color of the corn); "Treat one another with kindness, the trick is forgiveness" (use assorted candies on the board); "Forgiveness cemetery ... where Christians bury the faults of others" (create headstones with rhyming phrases that deal with concepts like lateness, fibbing, gossiping, messiness, absentmindedness, and bragging ... such as "Rest in peace, Sue's bragging tale, no power do you hold, God gives his promise, without fail, of treasure more than gold"); "Beware the devil's web: It's all tricks and no treats"

The Board

This board was covered with orange construction paper. The letters, with the exception of "tricks" and "treats," were cut from black construction paper. The word "beware" was hand-drawn in a drippy style to look creepy. "Tricks" and "treats" were made of light orange construction paper and mounted on a rectangle of black paper to insure that they were visible against the darker orange background. The spider web is a holiday decoration, obtained at a local store. It was hung by dental floss from the nail at the center of the bulletin board's frame. The spider is also a seasonal decoration. It is of the type made of cardboard and tissue paper. It came folded in half and the tissue-paper body of the spider puffed out when the spider was unfolded. It was purchased separately from the web (not the internet) and stapled onto the board. The staples on the spider help keep the spider web in place. Also fulfilling this function are the rubber spiders, purchased at a party store, which were stapled randomly on the web and across the board. One spider was tied to a piece of black yarn and was allowed to dangle freely down from the letter D in "devil."

November

Themes
Fall (again), Thanksgiving, hunting

Specific Phrases
"We are 'copiously' blessed" (create a giant cornucopia); "A thankful heart is a happy heart"; "It's hunting season, don't let Satan target you"

The Board
This bulletin board is simple to make, but deceptively expensive. The camouflage background with which the board was covered is burlap, obtained, as was the target, at a sporting goods store. The burlap was bought off a bolt by the yard and cost a total of about ten dollars. It was stapled across the top frame of the board and left to hang as it was, "camouflaging" the rectangular shape of the board. It was also stapled lightly along the side frame to prevent it from billowing out when people passed or doors were

51

opened. While the burlap was most effective, it was also pungent. If you fear that anyone in your church might be allergic or sensitive to so strong an odor, ordinary cloth of a similar pattern is available for purchase at fabric stores. It will, however, be even more expensive than the burlap and will not look quite as realistic. The small letters on the board were cut from deep orange construction paper, and the larger letters were made out of neon orange poster board. The board was completed by the addition of a strand of silk fall leaves obtained at a dollar store. The green plant visible in the picture, while it happens to go nicely with the bulletin board, is unrelated to the board.

December

Themes
Christmas, peace, brotherhood

Specific Phrases
"Wise men still seek him" (silhouette of Bethlehem with a star overhead); "Peace" (done in letters almost the height of the board, possibly stained-glass style); "Joy" (again oversized letters, this time with the Holy Family inside the letter *O*); "The greatest gift of all ... a Baby, a Son, a Savior"

The Board

Covered with bright red gift wrap, December's board has a shiny appearance which adds to its festive quality. The phrase, "The greatest gift of all" was cut from gold gift wrap. All the other letters were cut from copy paper, with each phrase increasing in size by one inch. The tree was made from two types of evergreen garland. The first type was the more realistic, stiffer, metal core variety. Instead of being a straight length of soft, fluffy green, it had individual small branches protruding from it and was more like a true evergreen swag would be. It was used to create the outline of the tree and to partially fill it.

Since the garland was wire-based, it was bendable, and since it had branches, there was no need to create a tree shape. Because of its thickness, the garland was mounted with a staple gun. It was formed into the shape of a triangle and the branches were bent and adjusted to give a more treelike appearance. Garland which was not used in creating the outline was zigzagged back and forth inside and fluffed up in the same manner as the outline. To cover any red background which might be peeking through, the second, softer garland was used. Since this standard variety is mostly fluff, it was easy to tuck it in and around the first garland. In some spots, it required no staples at all as it was held in place by the branches. In others, it was lightly stapled with a standard stapler.

Once the tree was completely filled with the green garland, a fancier, multicolored garland was zigzagged back and forth across the tree. It was held in place by the branches and required staples only at the edges where it changed direction. The little white ornaments are cotton balls to which drops of evergreen oil had been added so that the tree smelled like a tree. They stuck easily in the branches without requiring any method of attachment. The star is a lighted, flat-backed Christmas tree star which was hung on a nail specially added to the board's frame only for this occasion. If your board is not near an electrical outlet, any non-lighted decorative star would look just as nice.

Finally, the gifts were made of empty, small brown cardboard packing boxes. The short flaps on the boxes were closed first and the longer flaps were lapped over them. These flaps were not tucked in or sealed shut in any way. The boxes were then wrapped so that the flaps would be at the bottom of the package. Once the wrapping job was complete, the gifts were turned upside-down. An exacto knife was used to carefully cut the gift wrap along the three non-folded edges of one of the long flaps. This allowed the flap to be opened as an access point for stapling without damaging the appearance of a perfectly wrapped gift. The first box was mounted to the right of the tree. The box flap was opened so that the box was above and the flap hung down below. The gift-wrapped side of the flap was placed against the board. This flap was allowed to rest on the lower frame of the bulletin board for additional support. While the box was still open, the flap was liberally stapled using a staple gun. When the stapling was complete, the rest of the box was allowed to drop down into place, closing the box and hiding the stapling.

Two other boxes were mounted in the same fashion, one just to the right of the first box and one to the left of the tree. The final box was mounted in a similar manner, except that instead of resting on the bulletin board's frame, it rested on the two boxes below it. With loops of tape, bows were added to each of the boxes.

General Themes

No broad ideas will be listed here. There just isn't a simple method for categorizing creativity. When not tied down to a specific season, holiday, or event, your creativeness is limited only by the bounds of your imagination! Now is the chance to try out those catchy slogans you saw or to display your favorite scripture. There's no limit to what you can try! Instead, this section will simply include a selection of actual bulletin boards, each with its own unique theme. You might choose to recreate one of these. Or, they might serve to spark a new idea that's yours alone!

The Boards

Do not conform any longer to the pattern of this world ...
— Romans 12:2

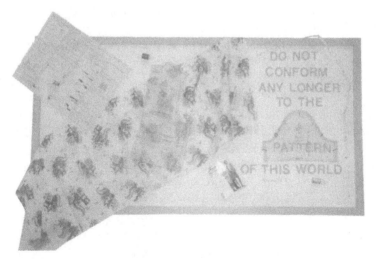

The starting point of this board was fabric. It was not bought for the board, but rather, happened to be on hand. Being bright and cheerful, it was a good choice to capture children's attention. The color schemes on the board were all based on the colors in the fabric. Obviously, the print of the fabric you choose will not be the same as the one shown here, so your color choices will be different. Here, a cotton blend was used. Cottons are fairly light, so they don't require more than an ordinary stapler to put them up. But they are heavy enough that, when hung doubled as this board's fabric was, they can't easily be seen through. Also, they don't stretch so they will retain their shape while hanging on a bulletin board.

White copy paper was used to cover this board for the simple reason that construction paper wasn't available at the time it was needed. While the copy paper served the purpose, construction paper would be a better choice as it is a little thicker and doesn't show through when it's overlapped. Next, the fabric was mounted on the board. When purchased at a fabric store, material comes off a bolt. At the factory, that fabric would have been put on the bolt so that it was folded in half lengthwise with the decorative or "right" side facing in. Once the fabric is cut off the bolt, you will need to turn it right-side-out before mounting it on the board. The fabric seen here had been turned and was placed lengthwise across the board while still folded in half.

How much fabric you will need to purchase will depend on the size of your bulletin board, however, two to two-and-a-half yards should be sufficient for most boards. One end of the fabric was stapled, with the folded side up, to the top of the board's frame (if you have a metal-framed board, tape will work), draped across the board and stapled just inside the edge of the frame's side. The ends of the fabric were allowed to hang freely. To the fabric was added a sheet of directions from a sewing pattern. You will not want to buy a pattern for this purpose. Any more, patterns cost upward of ten dollars. The investment would not be worthwhile. Instead, solicit a pattern from your congregation or from a home seamstress you might know. If you still come up empty-handed, try yard sales (if the season is right) or thrift stores. The sheet of directions on this board was placed in the upper left corner of the board. It served to cover an open expanse of board. As the directions slightly overlapped the fabric, the staple that held its lower right corner in place also helped to fasten the fabric to the board.

One large piece of the pattern was stapled lightly over the fabric. Another piece was stapled toward the lower right corner of the board. The phrase, "Do not conform any longer to the pattern of this world — Romans 12:2" was cut from green construction paper and stapled on the right end of the board so that the word "pattern" fell on the pattern piece.

Your lettering may take a slightly different arrangement depending on the size of your board and the size and shape of the pattern piece you have chosen to use. The addition of a few sewing supplies completed the board. The pattern sleeve (the envelope the pattern came in) was stapled to the board in an open spot near the bottom. A pair of sewing shears was added by threading string through the scissor's finger holes, tying it in a knot to make a loop, and hanging that loop over the center nail of the bulletin board.

Two spools of thread were also attached using string. Two pieces about twice the length of each spool were cut and a knot tied in one end of each. The unknotted ends were threaded through the holes in the spools, out the opposite ends, and knotted. The spools were mounted to the board by stapling the string to the board. For each of the four knots, a staple was placed on the string between the knot and the spool. The string supports the weight of the spool and the knot keeps the string from sliding through the staple.

Lastly, a tape measure was stapled to the board so that it snaked around the words and onto the fabric. If you can't obtain one of these at a dollar store, they are usually fairly inexpensive at fabric stores, or you can borrow one. No real harm will come to it except for the presence of a few small staple holes. Incidentally, the same can be said for the sewing pattern. If handled carefully, all of the pieces should be basically undamaged.

Don't masquerade as a Christian ... be one

    This bulletin board can be put up at any time of year. It could also be coordinated with the New Year (the idea of fresh starts) or with Mardi Gras. The background was covered with gift wrap. The paper used here was printed with gold stars, but any bright, non-holiday-specific paper would work. Draped across those ever-useful frame nails is a strand of extra-thick garland. This one happens to be gold, green, and purple, but what you use may depend upon what is available to you. The giant mask was cut from a single piece of metallic blue poster board. It was drawn freehand, using the same "arm as a compass" technique that was used to create the rainbow arcs on March's board.

    The two halves of the mask were made equal, except for a small tab sticking off one side near the top. This tab was later used as support for the stick to which a mask is attached. The eye holes were made identical by drawing (on the back of the mask) the size, shape, and location of one eye hole. This was cut out with an exacto knife. The resulting piece was used as a pattern for the other eye by placing the cutout in the desired location and tracing it. The stick that appears to support the mask is really a flag pole to which a small cloth flag was once attached. If you have access to any Fourth of July/Memorial Day decorations, this might be a good place to find a pole. A flag can be removed and reattached later. If you don't have such a source, don't limit your options by thinking strictly, "American flag." Many types of flags are popular right now, ranging from sports team flags to flags recognizing cultural heritage. These can be found in a wide variety of places. Don't forget to ask your congregation.

Once you have found your flag pole, the mask is then attached to the pole by wrapping the tab you made around the pole and fastening it against the back of the mask either with tape or staples. The purpose of this tab is for the mask to support the pole, not the other way around. The fan seen below the mask is really just a protective sleeve from a bunch of supermarket flowers. It was cut open along its seam. If, after looking and asking, you can't find a similar sleeve, you can make your own from any material of your choice: mylar, plastic, cloth, or gift wrap. The scalloped edge can be easily re-created by tracing the bottom of a drinking glass, moving the glass over, and tracing it again. This pattern is continued until the fan is wide enough for the needs of your board. The fan was stapled to the board so that it overlapped the flag pole. In addition to the staples required to hold the fan itself in place, staples were added to the fan along both sides of the flag pole. These, along with the mask's tab, helped support the flag pole and kept it in place. Next, the words, "Don't masquerade as a Christian ... be one" were added to the board. The words "masquerade" and "be one" were cut from red metallic poster board. The remainder of the words were cut in a smaller size from the same blue paper as was used for the large mask. Standard-sized party masks, available at a party supply store, were stapled randomly on the board and its frame.

Join us for Sunday school ... we're one "grape" bunch

Sunday school does not *have* to be the theme for this bulletin board. The phrase can be adapted for any group within your church like Bible study or youth group. The important thing is to choose the group you plan to feature, and then start early. Leave enough time to take pictures of the members of your group and have the film developed *before* this bulletin board needs to be put up. (If you have access to a digital camera and the knowledge of how to print digital pictures on a computer, both your preparation time and your cost can be cut down.) Once you have the pictures, the hardest part of the board is finding purple paper plates. They can be found in local chain stores, but you might have better luck at a party store which stocks paper goods in a rainbow of colors.

The bulletin board was covered with green felt just to provide a different texture, but this is not necessary. Felt is expensive and green paper will do the job nearly as well. If you decide to go with paper, try using a roll of fade-resistant bulletin board paper instead of construction paper. The colors are more vibrant than ordinary construction paper, and, as the name suggests, the color holds up well. The letters for the board were all cut from purple construction paper with the exception of the word, "grape," which was cut from glossy purple poster board.

Draped across the frame nails are two strands of silk grape vines, purchased at a dollar store. The end of each strand was hooked on the center frame nail and the vines were extended in opposite directions, draped over the board's corner nails, and allowed to dangle down the side of the bulletin board. To these vines were added a few bunches of rubber grapes which were stapled on with a staple gun. Thrift stores, yard sales, craft stores, and your congregation are all possible sources for artificial grapes. So that all the "visual activity" doesn't occur just on the upper portion of the board, a bunch of grapes was stapled to both of the board's lower corners.

The paper plates were added, by standard stapler, to the bulletin board in a fashion which suggested a bunch of grapes. How many plates you use and the exact arrangement of them will be determined by both the size of your board and the size of the plates you are using. *This* board required twenty paper plates. Finally, photographs were stapled onto the paper plates. Everyone seems to love seeing their picture on display. Don't forget that children are short. While it might be a slightly less aesthetically pleasing arrangement, you might want to consider putting a larger number of photographs lower down on the grape bunch so that even the littlest children can see them.

Top ten on God's chart

For children who are growing up with computer chips, CDs, and DVDs, this bulletin is about as antique as the first stone wheel. Yet, perhaps for that very reason, children seem attracted to the board. For those old enough to remember 45s, its nostalgic appeal is unquestionable. In short, it seems to be a bulletin board that is appreciated by almost everyone. The keystone of this bulletin board is a large plastic record which was purchased inexpensively at a party store. The song title on the record was covered over. Using glue and a color of paper similar to the record label, the title "The Ten Commandments" was added.

Twelve additional records were created from construction paper. For each record, two large sheets of black construction paper were slightly overlapped and glued together. When the glue was dry, a large round serving plate was traced onto the paper and the resulting circle was cut out. To make each record label, a small sheet of colored construction paper was used. A salad-sized plate was traced and the circle it created was cut out. In the middle of this circle was placed a small drinking glass. Its bottom was traced to create the hole in the middle of the label. This smaller circle can be cut either with scissors or an exacto knife. The completed label was then glued onto the black record. For the purpose of variety, records were made with different colored labels. You can choose those colors which appeal to you.

The second key component of this bulletin board is a preprinted set of cards bearing the Ten Commandments. These were also obtained, surprisingly, at a party store. While having professionally made cards is attractive, it is not necessary. With access to a computer, you can create a set of your own in any size and color you choose. In fact, this method gives you more creative flexibility. By being able to manipulate the size of the commandments, you have better control over what goes where on the board and how well it fits. While you're at your computer, you might want to go ahead and print the board's slogan, "Top ten on God's chart."

Unless the computer you're using has the capability to print banners, you will need to print your letters and words on separate pages and glue these pages together when you're done. Ordinarily, this type of lettering gives a less-polished appearance to a bulletin board. In *this* case, the board is so active that the white copy paper serves to connect the words and highlight the phrase. The last thing you'll want to print are the numbers one through ten. Again, the white background will serve to make the numbers stand out. To assemble the bulletin board, first cover it with construction paper in a color of your choice. Purple was used here. Next, center the plastic disc on the board. As the record was really designed to be a party decoration, it should have a little hole or tab by which it was intended to be suspended. A thumbtack through this hole should provide plenty of support for the record. Next, decide where you plan to place each of the Ten Commandments. One construction paper record will go with each commandment. Don't forget that either the commandments, or the records, or both, can extend beyond the edge of the board.

When you have decided on placement, staple the records and commandments to the board. Remember that the whole record or the whole paper sheet doesn't have to show. In fact, with the number of items you will be adding to this board, it is more than likely that you will want to overlap some things. Once the commandments and their records are in place, get a glue stick and the numbers you made. Now that you can see where everything has been placed, you can choose the best spot on each record for its corresponding number. Using the glue stick, add the numbers. Now staple the eleventh and twelfth record at the top and bottom of the board, extending them beyond the board's frame, you will want to use a loop of tape on the upper back of these records. The tape will keep the top of the record from drooping down over the board.

Finally, complete the board by adding some musical notes. The ones seen here were cut from construction paper scraps left over when the records were cut out. The size of your board and the amount of space left on it will determine the size and number of notes you will want to add. These notes can be drawn freehand, using the picture as a guide. Once you have drawn one note, you can cut it out and use it as a pattern. To save time and effort, you can also stack the paper scraps and cut out more than one note at a time.

The Fun Begins

So you survived all that reading! The question is, did you learn anything? Hopefully, your mind is a-whirl with possibilities for creating your own unique bulletin boards. At the very least you should have found an idea which will cover up the blank cork board for which you're responsible!

What now? Let your imagination run wild. Accept suggestions. Be open to inspiration. Get excited about your board and its message. When you do, it will show in the finished product. And you never know, great things may happen! Your small message in paper and staples may affect someone as profoundly as any inspiring sermon.

Happy creating and God bless.

Rosalind M. Townley